A MESSAGE TO PARENTS

Reading good books to young children is a crucial factor in a child's psychological and intellectual development. It promotes a mutually warm and satisfying relationship between parent and child and enhances the child's awareness of the world around him. It stimulates the child's imagination and lays a foundation for the development of the skills necessary to support the critical thinking process. In addition, the parent who reads to his child helps him to build vocabulary and other prerequisite skills for the child's own successful reading.

In order to provide parents and children with books which will do these things, Brown Watson has published this series of small books specially designed for young children. These books are factual, fanciful, humorous, questioning and adventurous. A library acquired in this inexpensive way will provide many hours of pleasurable and profitable reading for parents and children.

This edition first published 2001 by
Brown Watson, England

Cinderella

Text by Maureen Spurgeon

Brown Watson

ENGLAND

Once, Cinderella and her father, the Baron, had lived alone, after the death of her mother when she was a baby. She loved him dearly.

How she sighed, remembering those happy days before her father married a widow with two daughters of her own.

The widow's daughters were so ugly and cruel, they quickly became known as The Ugly Sisters.

Soon, the Baron's daughter was made to do all the housework.

She was dressed in rags, and because she spent so much time in the kitchen among the cinders, they called her "Cinderella".

Then, one morning, Cinderella heard a loud knock at the door.

It was a message from the royal palace, sent to all the houses in the kingdom.

"Invitations to a Grand Ball in honour of the Prince Charming" squealed the Ugly Sisters.

Cinderella's heart began to beat.

She ran up the cellar steps, almost bumping into the Baron!

"Father!" she panted, "the invitations that have come for the Grand Ball! I can go, can't I?"

But before the Baron could answer, Cinderella's step-mother shouted out:

"You? Go to the Ball dressed in your rags? Talk sense, Cinderella! You're only fit to stay at home!"

Cinderella knew the Baron was too afraid of his wife to say anything. The Ugly Sisters were delighted, glad of an excuse to make Cinderella work harder than ever.

"Alter my dress!" "Brush my hair!" "Shine my shoes!" "Iron my gloves!"

They meant to look their very best for the handsome Prince Charming.

By the evening of the Ball, Cinderella was so unhappy she could hardly bear it. Alone in the house, she sat by the fire, her tears falling into the cold, black cinders.

Then, a dazzling glow of light seemed to fill the kitchen, making it bright and warm.

"Do not cry, Cinderella", came a soft voice. "I am here to help you."

"H — help me?" Cinderella stammered. "But, how? Who — who are you?"

"Your Fairy Godmother," came the reply. "And with my magic wand, I shall see that you go to the Ball!"

Before Cinderella could answer, her Fairy Godmother gave a tap with her wand — and, in an instant, her rags became the most beautiful ball gown she could ever have imagined!

"I shall need a pumpkin . . ." said the Fairy Godmother.

"There's one in the kitchen garden . . ." said Cinderella.

The Fairy Godmother turned a fat pumpkin into a crystal coach! Four mice became white ponies, and two rats were changed into footmen!

"Thank you, Fairy Godmother!" cried Cinderella.

"Just remember my magic can only last until midnight!" her Godmother smiled.

Well, what a stir when
Cinderella arrived at the Palace!
Everyone wanted to know who
the beautiful young girl was —
including Prince Charming, who
at once came up to her.

They danced the whole evening, falling in love with each hour that slipped by.

The Ugly Sisters had no idea that the beautiful girl was Cinderella!

On the first stroke of midnight,
Cinderella remembered what her
Fairy Godmother had said.
"I — I have to go!" she cried, and
turned to run down the stairs.

Prince Charming was surprised and knew he had to see the beautiful girl again.

The only clue she left was a tiny, glass slipper . . .

There was great excitement next day. A royal procession came around all the streets, with a page carrying the glass slipper on a red cushion.

"Whoever this slipper fits," said the Royal Herald, "shall marry Prince Charming!"

"It will fit me!" squealed the first Ugly Sister. "It will fit me!"

"No, me!" screamed her sister.

But, the slipper was much too small for either of them.

"But, this is the last house!" cried the Herald. "Is there nobody else?"

"Only my daughter," said the Baron quickly. "I'll call her."

And even before he put the slipper on Cinderella's tiny foot, the Prince knew she was the girl he loved.

A MESSAGE TO PARENTS

Reading good books to young children is a crucial factor in a child's psychological and intellectual development. It promotes a mutually warm and satisfying relationship between parent and child and enhances the child's awareness of the world around him. It stimulates the child's imagination and lays a foundation for the development of the skills necessary to support the critical thinking process. In addition, the parent who reads to his child helps him to build vocabulary and other prerequisite skills for the child's own successful reading.

In order to provide parents and children with books which will do these things, Brown Watson has published this series of small books specially designed for young children. These books are factual, fanciful, humourous, questioning and adventurous. A library acquired in this inexpensive way will provide many hours of pleasurable and profitable reading for parents and children.

Cinderella

Text by Maureen Spurgeon

Brown Watson

ENGLAND

Art and text copyright © 1990 Brown Watson Ltd. England.
Printed and bound in Belgium.
STARTRIGHT ELF and the Startright Elf logo are trademarks of
Checkerboard Press, Inc. USA. 0 9 8 7 6 5 4 3 2 1

Once, Cinderella and her father, the Baron, had lived alone, after the death of her mother when she was a baby. She loved him dearly.

How she sighed, remembering those happy days before her father married a widow with two daughters of her own.

The widow's daughters were so ugly and cruel, they quickly became known as The Ugly Sisters.

Soon, the Baron's daughter was made to do all the housework.

She was dressed in rags, and because she spent so much time in the kitchen among the cinders, they called her "Cinderella".

Then, one morning, Cinderella
heard a loud knock at the door.

It was a message from the royal
palace, sent to all the houses in
the kingdom.

"Invitations to a Grand Ball in honour of the Prince Charming" squealed the Ugly Sisters.

Cinderella's heart began to beat.

She ran up the cellar steps, almost bumping into the Baron!

"Father!" she panted, "the invitations that have come for the Grand Ball! I can go, can't I?"

But before the Baron could
answer, Cinderella's step-mother
shouted out:

"You? Go to the Ball dressed in
your rags? Talk sense, Cinderella!
You're only fit to stay at home!"

Cinderella knew the Baron was too afraid of his wife to say anything. The Ugly Sisters were delighted, glad of an excuse to make Cinderella work harder than ever.

"Alter my dress!" "Brush my hair!" "Shine my shoes!" "Iron my gloves!"

They meant to look their very best for the handsome Prince Charming.

By the evening of the Ball, Cinderella was so unhappy she could hardly bear it. Alone in the house, she sat by the fire, her tears falling into the cold, black cinders.

Then, a dazzling glow of light seemed to fill the kitchen, making it bright and warm.

"Do not cry, Cinderella", came a soft voice. "I am here to help you."

"H – help me?" Cinderella stammered. "But, how? Who – who are you?"

"Your Fairy Godmother," came the reply. "And with my magic wand, I shall see that you go to the Ball!"

Before Cinderella could answer, her Fairy Godmother gave a tap with her wand — and, in an instant, her rags became the most beautiful ball gown she could ever have imagined!

"I shall need a pumpkin . . ." said the Fairy Godmother.

"There's one in the kitchen garden . . ." said Cinderella.

The Fairy Godmother turned a fat pumpkin into a crystal coach! Four mice became white ponies, and two rats were changed into footmen!

"Thank you, Fairy Godmother!" cried Cinderella.

"Just remember my magic can only last until midnight!" her Godmother smiled.

Well, what a stir when Cinderella arrived at the Palace! Everyone wanted to know who the beautiful young girl was — including Prince Charming, who at once came up to her.

They danced the whole evening, falling in love with each hour that slipped by.

The Ugly Sisters had no idea that the beautiful girl was Cinderella!

On the first stroke of midnight, Cinderella remembered what her Fairy Godmother had said.

"I — I have to go!" she cried, and turned to run down the stairs.

Prince Charming was surprised and knew he had to see the beautiful girl again.

The only clue she left was a tiny, glass slipper . . .

There was great excitement
next day. A royal procession
came around all the streets, with a
page carrying the glass slipper on
a red cushion.

"Whoever this slipper fits," said the Royal Herald, "shall marry Prince Charming!"

"It will fit me!" squealed the first Ugly Sister. "It will fit me!"

"No, me!" screamed her sister.

But, the slipper was much too small for either of them.

"But, this is the last house!" cried the Herald. "Is there nobody else?"

"Only my daughter," said the Baron quickly. "I'll call her."

And even before he put the slipper on Cinderella's tiny foot, the Prince knew she was the girl he loved.